Surprising Things

We Eat

Monika Davies

Consultants

Timothy Rasinski, Ph.D.
Kent State University

Lori Oczkus, M.A.
Literacy Consultant

Kent Truog
Documentary Filmmaker

Publishing Credits

Rachelle Cracchiolo, M.S.Ed., *Publisher*
Conni Medina, M.A.Ed., *Managing Editor*
Dona Herweck Rice, *Series Developer*
Emily R. Smith, M.A.Ed., *Content Director*
Stephanie Bernard/Noelle Cristea, M.A.Ed., *Editors*
Robin Erickson, *Senior Graphic Designer*

The TIME logo is a registered trademark of TIME Inc. Used under license.

Image Credits: Cover and p. 1 Westend61 GmbH/Alamy Stock Photo; pp. 4-5 aluxum/iStock.com; p. 6 (bottom right) MAHATHIR MOHD YASIN/Shutterstock.com; p. 7 Peter Horree/Alamy Stock Photo; p. 10 Michael Spring/Dreamstime.com; p. 11 Bhofack2/Dreamstime.com; pp. 12-13 Shanti Hesse/Shutterstock.com; p. 14 (left) Agcuesta/Dreamstime.com, (right) Pcphotography69/Dreamstime.com; p. 24 Paul Rushton/Alamy Stock Photo; p. 26 Peter Stuckings/Shutterstock.com; p. 27 imageBROKER/Alamy Stock Photo; p. 28 Andreas Rentz/Getty Images; p. 31 Bhofack2/Dreamstime.com; p. 32 Charles Phoenix; p. 33 Courtesy of Çırağan Palace Kempinski Istanbul; p. 34 Richard Lim/Alamy Stock Photo; p. 35 Neil Setchfield/Alamy Stock Photo; p. 39 Ires007/Dreamstime.com; p. 41 Richard Splash/Alamy Stock Photo; p. 42 Oli Scarff/Getty Images; pp. 44-45 Neil Setchfield/Alamy Stock Photo; p. 46 Irene Tong/Flickr License: Creative Commons BY-SA 2.0; pp. 48, 50 Sue Hwang; pp. 49 (top), 55 Jim Behymer; p. 49 (second image from bottom) Bill Hinton Photography/Getty Images, (bottom) Courtesy of Marisa Niederreither; all other images from iStock and/or Shutterstock

Library of Congress Cataloging-in-Publication Data

Names: Davies, Monika, author.
Title: Surprising things we eat / Monika Davies.
Description: Huntington Beach, CA : Teacher Created Materials, [2017] | Audience: Grades 7 to 8. | Includes index.
Identifiers: LCCN 2016052265 (print) | LCCN 2016055189 (ebook) | ISBN 9781493836376 (pbk.) | ISBN 9781480757417 (eBook)
Subjects: LCSH: Food--Juvenile literature.
Classification: LCC TX355 .D3427 2017 (print) | LCC TX355 (ebook) | DDC 641.3--dc23
LC record available at https://lccn.loc.gov/2016052265

Teacher Created Materials

5301 Oceanus Drive
Huntington Beach, CA 92649-1030
http://www.tcmpub.com

ISBN 978-1-4938-3637-6
© 2017 Teacher Created Materials, Inc.

Open Minds, Full Stomachs

While you're reading, consider the stories behind the food you eat on a day-to-day basis. Consider how you could incorporate new and exciting ingredients into your next meal. "You are what you eat," the saying goes. What does the food on your plate say about you?

There's no better way to dive right into the heart of a city than by trying its food. Picking out food in a new country will always lead you to surprises—the best part of any journey.

Japan

Japan has a reputation for harboring some of the most unusual (and tastiest) foods you will ever encounter. Here are some highlights from a grocery store in this country.

Tuna Eyeball

There's nothing quite like having a staring contest with your next meal! Tuna eyeballs are a common **staple** on Japanese grocery shelves.

Wasp Crackers

Scamper over to Omachi, Japan, for this stinger of a treat. Wasp crackers are rice crackers filled with wasps, which taste like slightly bitter raisins.

Cherry Blossom Meat

If you are a fan of sushi joints, you are probably familiar with sashimi (raw fish or meat). Cherry blossom meat is quite different from the average ocean-bred sashimi, as this extremely red variety is actually raw horsemeat.

Kit Kats®

Kit Kats are hugely popular in Japan, and as such, your choices for Kit Kat flavors are decidedly more varied. Keep an eye out for Kit Kats with unique tastes, such as green tea, soy bean, and baked potato . . . just to name a few!

自家特製品 アイスボックスにて お届けします

地方発送承ります

電話ハガキ注文OK 打田

本日の 太巻

本日の 太巻

Seasonal Flavors

In Japan, a lot of importance is placed on serving food of the freshest quality and what is seasonally available. That means you will find Japanese supermarkets stocked with fruits and vegetables that are currently being harvested. For example, delicious strawberries line the shelves from December to May, but you may need to pick another fruit during the rest of the year.

7

Food Expenses in Different Countries

How much do people around the world spend on food? Have a look at the data on these pages and compare the numbers.

Country	Percentage of household income spent on food
United States	6.5
Japan	13.5
Brazil	15.6
China	25.5
Kenya	46.9

Source: USDA, Economic Research Service

ALASKA
UNITED STATES OF AMERICA

CANADA

UNITED STATES OF AMERICA

MEXICO

Things to Consider

◎ For each country, compare the amount of money spent on groceries per person with the percentage of household income spent on food. What do you notice?

◎ What factors may be responsible for the differences in these numbers?

◎ Do these numbers surprise you? Why or why not?

VENEZUELA
COLOMBIA
ECUADOR
PERU
BOLIVIA
BRAZIL
PARAGUAY
ARGENTINA
CHILE
URUGUAY

Amount of Money Spent on Groceries (per person, U.S. dollars)—2008

Source: Washington State University, 2008

Iceland

A country of glaciers, volcanoes, and puffins, Iceland is well known for some fascinating food items that can be found on its grocery store shelves.

Kæstur Hákarl (Fermented Shark)

Fresh basking shark is poisonous. To get around this, Icelanders bury the caught shark and let it **ferment** for 6–12 weeks. Once the aged shark has been fermented, it's dried and served. Tasting of rotten cheese and smelling strongly of ammonia, *kæstur hákarl* is definitely not for the easily queasy.

Rúgbrauð (Hot Springs Rye Bread)

Rúgbrauð is a sweet, dark rye bread made out of simple ingredients and a baking twist. Traditionally, this bread is baked in a special pot buried in the ground near a hot spring, yielding a distinct flavor.

A Viking Diet

When the Vikings first settled in Iceland, the basking shark was a common source of meat found in the waters; unfortunately, it is toxic to humans. Through a pretty tough trial and error, the Vikings discovered that fermentation was the key to eating shark, and *kæstur hákarl* was born.

Sviò (Sheep's Head)

People are divided on what the best part of the sheep is: the tongue, the cheek, or the eyes. Most Icelanders agree that sheep's head is a beloved traditional **delicacy**. You will probably like *sviò*, if you can stomach your food looking at you.

Harðfiskur (Fish Jerky)

Add salted butter to soften and moisten *harðfiskur* and you have Icelanders' favorite snack. The most popular versions are cod and haddock, and this snack is Iceland's version of the more well-known beef variety.

Iceland

Try Skyr

Do you want a taste of Iceland that is a bit more . . . subtle? Try *skyr*, the Icelandic version of yogurt, and—arguably—the best and healthiest yogurt in the world. While it is technically Icelandic cheese created out of skim milk, it is marketed as yogurt in grocery stores in the United States.

Thailand

Local food markets in Thailand are kaleidoscopes of pop-up street vendors, overwhelming smells, and colorful dishes full of character—perfect places for curious explorers.

Durian

The durian is a spiky, stinky fruit. It is infamous for its smell, which has been compared to sweaty socks. As long as you do not judge the durian solely by its smell, you may find yourself rewarded with a taste of the fruit's sweet, buttery custard.

A Spoon and Fork, Please

If you find yourself in Thailand, the spoon may become your favorite utensil. The Thai use their spoons more than their forks, which are just there to lift food onto the spoons.

Fried Grasshoppers

These crispy critters can be found at most food markets. The grasshoppers offer a source of protein, and many think they taste like chicken.

Luk Chup (Thai Marzipan)

The glossy and brightly colored *luk chup* is marzipan with a Thai spin. These adorable candies are made out of mung beans, coconut milk, and sugar. They are often shaped into tiny fruits and vegetables and will **wholly** satisfy your sweet tooth.

Bread, Bread, Bread

Bread is a staple in food diets around the world, and people from all over the world have put their own spins on the grain product.

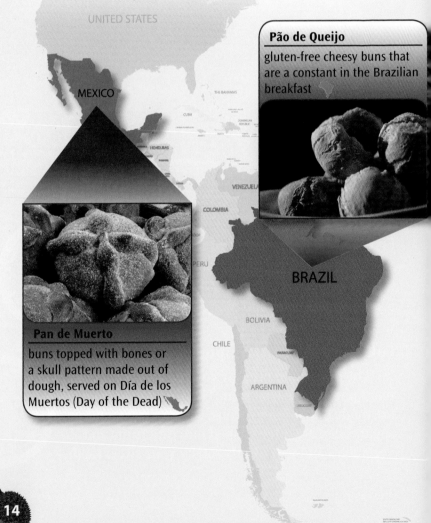

Pão de Queijo

gluten-free cheesy buns that are a constant in the Brazilian breakfast

Pan de Muerto

buns topped with bones or a skull pattern made out of dough, served on Día de los Muertos (Day of the Dead)

RUSSIA

Bauernbrot

chewy sourdough rye bread
traditionally made only of
water, flour, yeast, and salt

INDIA

Naan

a versatile flatbread, usually
cooked in a tandoor oven,
which captures hearts in parts
of Asia

Baguette

the iconic and crusty bread
that is undoubtedly as French
as the Eiffel Tower

Things to Consider

- Look into the history behind
  each bread item. What is the
  cultural importance of the
  bread to each country?

- For what reasons might bread
  be a staple in most countries?

15

Eccentric Ingredient Profiles

When was the last time you really leapt out of your ingredient comfort zone? Here are introductions from a few **unconventional** ingredients that you have likely never met. Give them a fair chance in your next recipe. You won't be disappointed!

Pandan Leaves

I will color your world a fluorescent lime hue.

Seeking. . .

I'd love to find a recipe that doesn't mind if I turn everything green.

My Life Story

I'm usually found hanging out in Malaysian and Indonesian kitchens, though I have migrated over to America. You will typically find me buddied up with dessert recipes.

I'm all about big flavor, and I'm known for imparting a floral sweetness to recipes. You can buy me fresh (perfect for **savory** dishes), frozen (a handy substitute if you cannot find fresh leaves), or as a canned **extract** (specifically for desserts).

Where Can I Find Pandan Leaves?

Many Asian grocery stores stock pandan leaves, and you can also purchase them online through several vendors. Be careful, though, and avoid anything labeled as "pandan flavoring." You will want fresh leaves or genuine extract to dodge disappointment when creating your next pandan-inspired recipe.

An Essential Ingredient

Pandan leaves grow in abundance in Thailand and are an important ingredient in Southeast Asian **cuisine** as they add great flavor and are inexpensive. Pandan leaves are also woven into baskets, act as insect repellent, and are occasionally used in perfume. Talk about a multitasker!

My Successful Matches

If you're still not sold on me as a potential ingredient, here's my résumé of successful taste matches:

- *Pandan waffles:* crispy waffles with a moist green center

- *Pandan cake:* sweet, fluffy delight that mixes a floral pandan taste with coconut

- *Onde-onde:* dumplings made of pandan leaves, palm sugar, and coconut

- *Pandan chicken:* chicken wrapped in fragrant pandan leaves

Dragon Fruit (Pitaya)

As long as you do not chew my flashy shell, we'll get along just swell.

Seeking. . .

I'm looking for new friends to take a chance on me.

My Life Story

Am I a pineapple dipped into radioactive pink batter or a mixed-up poppy seed cake trapped inside a bitter shell? Sadly, neither description quite captures my true essence. I am a tropical fruit native to Mexico, Central America, and South America with a pretty wild wardrobe, a high dose of antioxidants, and a fiber-rich attitude. Trust me, I'm a fruit you should get to know better.

You can absolutely dine on me without adding me to a recipe. All you have to do is cut me lengthwise, scoop out my interior, and then make sure you peel off any pieces of my bitter pink shell. I'm not an overdose of sweetness but taste like a pear and kiwi blended together.

If you're feeling adventurous, check out my successful matches for a few different recipes that have made me an all-star!

My Successful Matches

- *Dragon fruit smoothies*
- *Dragon fruit pancakes*
- *Dragon fruit jelly mooncakes*
- *Dragon fruit sorbet*
- *Dragon fruit cheesecake*

Choose Perfect Dragon Fruit

Make sure you select a dragon fruit with an evenly colored shell. Next, check the dragon fruit's stem, and ensure it is slightly pliable, not **brittle** to the touch. If you gently press the dragon fruit and find it gives slightly, that's a good indication the fruit is not overripe.

19

Worcestershire Sauce

Hard to say, easy to eat.

Seeking. . .

I'm a flexible sauce compatible with a whole **array** of recipes.

My Life Story

You should know that my backstory is not a pretty tale. Essentially, I come to life with the help of fermented anchovies—itty-bitty saltwater fish kept in vinegar for about 18 months. Add in some onions, molasses, corn syrup, salt, garlic, and a few other spices, and *voilà*! Worcestershire sauce comes to life and is subsequently capped away into a bottle.

I can understand if you're feeling timid about adding me to a recipe, especially since I sound like old fish juice. I'd recommend you give me a chance though, as I'm very capable of adding a bold, meaty flavor to a variety of dishes.

Worcestershire's Origin Story

In the 1800s, a nobleman who had recently returned from travels in Bengal asked two chemists to re-create a sauce he'd enjoyed on his journey. The initial creation by chemists John Lea and William Perrins was not to their liking and was shelved. A couple of years later, they rediscovered the sauce, which had become a savory delight. The most widely known Worcestershire sauce, the Lea & Perrins® version, was officially born.

My Successful Matches

- *Marinades:* Instead of soy sauce, use Worcestershire sauce as a way to give flavor to an otherwise flavorless dishes in your life.

- *Hearty meat dishes:* Start preparing hamburgers, stews, chili, and other hearty dishes with a dose of Worcestershire sauce. The sauce will enhance the flavors in these meat-heavy dishes.

- *Caesar salad dressing:* Good old Worcestershire is a popular seasoning for this dressing.

My Snack-tastic Road Trip

A Food Diary Inspired by Your Author's Travels

For two summers, I worked a job where I spent all day folding shirts, but I saved my nickels and dimes and purchased a plane ticket to see the world. In my hands was a bucket list of places I had been itching to see and cities with food I had always been curious to try. I am a huge fan of street food, and I was determined to try everything—the sweet treats, the weird-smelling dishes, and the gross-out snacks. I was familiar with the old adage "You are what you eat," and I remember wondering whether trying new food would change my **perspective** of this world. (Spoiler alert: It most certainly did.)

Join me on my road trip down memory lane, and let's breathe in the sights and smells of the different street foods around the world.

street food vendor in Bangkok, Thailand

THINK LINK

- Why do you think people find street food appealing?

- Why would the author assume there would be gross-out snacks on the trip? What makes the author describe them as such?

Hong Kong, China

I jetted to Hong Kong first, a city that hustles and bustles and glows neon in the night. I had just narrowly avoided paying too much for a knockoff Rolex™ watch when a sweet smell and a small crowd drew my attention. A food vendor was wielding a very strange waffle iron. A satisfied customer walked past me, and I glimpsed what he was holding—the tastiest bubble wrap I had ever seen in my life.

I had officially met the egg waffle (*gai daan tsai*), one of the shining stars of Hong Kong's street-food scene. The waffle has a collection of small, egg-like bubbles bonded together, just like golden bubble wrap. Immediately after purchasing one, I bit in—and found the waffle to be a crispy delight on the outside with a sweet, soft center.

My **hostel**'s receptionist told me Hong Kong is known as the "World's Food Fair," and that stayed in my mind as I tried chicken feet, shrimp dumplings, milk tea, and five helpings of egg waffles. Soon, I had started to master the art of chopsticks and began ordering tea with my meals, just like the locals. My journey had officially begun, and I felt my worldview expanding.

Who Invented the Egg Waffle?

There is a lot of dispute about the egg waffle's origin. Some people think that these uniquely shaped egg waffles were made in the 1950s to make up for the eggless batter that was common after World War II. Others say street vendors came up with the iconic waffle as a way to use broken eggs.

Skuon, Cambodia

A couple days later, I worked my way down to Southeast Asia—and found myself engulfed and overwhelmed by cultural differences. I took the train through Vietnam, spent hours staring at the sea, and then entered Cambodia, a land of dust, palm trees, and hardworking people.

The prices of everything were astonishingly low, and I was able to dine like royalty for less than $3. However, the poverty in Cambodia made me think of how lucky I am never to have experienced hunger and to have a job that pays me more than $5 a day.

As I left Cambodia's capital, Phnom Penh, by bus, I stopped in Skuon. Several women with large baskets approached me as I exited the bus. They carried Skuon's delicacy—fried spiders (*a-ping*). A vendor encouraged me to go for the crispiest one and to try the legs first.

Why Spiders?

There is no clear reason why Cambodians began the practice of eating fried spiders. But many people believe the practice was a result of the lack of food during the Khmer Rouge regime (1975–79). During this tragic era, about 1.5 million Cambodians, out of a total population of 7 million, were executed or died of starvation and disease.

The fried spider was coated in oil, salt, and sugar. I was a little hesitant, but I began to chew the crispy "treat." Surprisingly, the taste turned a bit nutty once I reached the center.

As I left, head pressed against a dusty bus window, I couldn't stop thinking about how unforgettable this taste of Cambodia's culture had been.

Eat a Spider, Grow . . . Healthy Hair?

Need another reason to try a spider? Cambodian women believe that eating these crunchy treats makes you beautiful and that the spider is specifically responsible for helping grow thick, healthy hair.

LUXUSVARIANTE
LUXURY

Für die ganz speziellen
Luxusvariante der Currywur
Champagner serviert.
For the very special
with gold leaf, served w

CHE VARIA
RICAL

durch die Einführung der kosta
plexer ist die Darreichung der Cu
chon eine alte Tradition. Heute wir
n selten so serviert.
nally currywurst was served wit
ave largely disappeared since
er plastic variety.

A Delicious Museum

There is an entire museum in Berlin
dedicated to bringing the smell, taste, and
feel of the currywurst to life for locals and
tourists. A ticket to the Deutsches Currywurst
Museum includes a sampler of currywurst, as
well as access to interactive exhibits.

28

Berlin, Germany

When I entered Germany, I headed straight to Berlin, a city steeped in history I had only heard about in my social studies classroom.

A food stand caught my eye on my walk back from the Reichstag building. The vendor was handing out bunless hot dogs that appeared to be drowning in some kind of red sauce. I discovered I had unwittingly stumbled upon the snack staple of Germany's capital—currywurst.

The chatty vendor told me of the snack's invention. According to the tale, Herta Heuwer created the delicious snack in 1949 after getting ketchup, Worcestershire sauce, and curry powder from British soldiers. She combined the three ingredients and poured the **concoction** over a grilled sausage. This officially brought currywurst into existence. The snack was an immediate success due to the pop of flavor—as well as how the hearty snack fills hungry stomachs.

The currywurst is the hot dog I never knew I needed. Before I left to take the train to Frankfurt, I snagged one more for the ride.

The Currywurst Utensil

To eat a currywurst properly, make sure to pick up a currywurst fork. This utensil is a small plastic or wooden fork and makes eating on the go easy!

Vancouver, Canada

My last stop on this adventure was the seasonally cold terrain of Canada, my home. I flew to Vancouver, a city bordered with snow-capped mountains and a deep, clear river. I admit that the city does feel remarkably similar to America. However, we Canadians use a "loonie" coin instead of a dollar bill, are mildly obsessed with a fast-food chain named Tim Hortons, and tend to apologize a lot.

I was avoiding the Vancouver rain when I decided to finally try **poutine**, the **quintessential** Canadian dish. Originating in rural Quebec (a Canadian province), this unique take on fries covered in cheese and gravy has always made me raise my eyebrows.

Canadians are always on the search to stay warm, and suddenly, the popularity of poutine began to make sense. Not only did it taste delicious, but it also was served piping hot, and it warmed me up.

I began the trek back home to my part of Canada. Once there, I unpacked memories and the scents and smells of new places and perspectives, the taste of a good trip still lingering.

Double Double

There's a lot of common Canadian lingo that has never crossed the border into other countries. When ordering at Tim Hortons, Canadians will often order a "double double." This is Canadian code for two creams and two sugars in a cup of coffee.

PINpoint Your Sweet Tooth

People around the world have found unique ways to satisfy their cravings for sweets, and we have pinned some of our delectable favorites. See if there's a dessert you might want to taste test!

Cakes

Cherpumple

If you are looking to have it all, allow us to introduce you to what could be your new favorite dessert—the Cherpumple! This **scrumptious** delight contains cherry, pumpkin, and apple pie, all held together with yellow cake and spice cake. Charles Phoenix, an American comic, designed the recipe when he was faced with too many delicious options at his Thanksgiving dessert table. Talk about a one-stop dessert!

Charles Phoenix (American Humorist)
The "Turducken" of Cakes

32

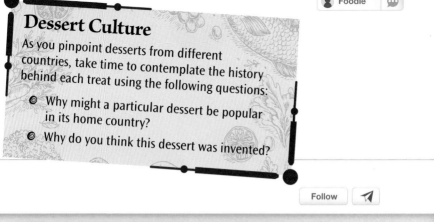

Dessert Culture

As you pinpoint desserts from different countries, take time to contemplate the history behind each treat using the following questions:

- Why might a particular dessert be popular in its home country?
- Why do you think this dessert was invented?

Follow

Sultan's Golden Cake

It may look like a solid bar of gold, but this is an **edible** masterpiece . . . with a price tag to match its golden looks! Served at Istanbul's Çırağan Palace Kempinski Hotel, this cake takes 72 hours to create. The Golden Cake is whipped together with apricots, **quinces**, figs, and pears that have been swimming in Jamaican rum for two years. Covered with a topping consisting of caramel, black truffles, and real gold leaf, this $1,000 dessert "takes the cake"!

Çırağan Palace Kempinski Hotel (Istanbul, Turkey)

Courtly Cakes

Fried Wonders

Picarones

Don't be fooled by the doughnutlike appearance of the picarones—the Peruvian delights have their own flair. Picarones are filled with a **puree** of squash and sweet potato to give them a uniquely spicy, sweet flavor. Topped with *chancaca* syrup, they will leave you with sweet dreams.

 **Peru,
South America**
Funky Fritters

Martabak Manis

These are not your regular Sunday pancakes. Found at food stalls all around Indonesia, *martabak manis* is first created in special pans and layered with butter. The customer's choice of toppings follows (chocolate and cheese being typical choices). The vendor artfully folds the layers together, cutting the dessert into sandwich-like squares. Try just one bite, and you are guaranteed to finish the rest!

 **Indonesia,
Southeast Asia**
Plucky Pancakes

Fried Mars Bar

**Scotland,
United Kingdom**
Upgraded Candy Bars

Deep-Fried Mars® Bar

The deep-fried Mars bar is now a worldwide sensation, but it is said to have come into existence because of a bet. As the story goes, in a chip shop in Scotland (serving takeaway fish and chips), one man bet his friend that he wouldn't eat a Mars bar tossed in a deep fryer—the rest is high-calorie history. It is now a popular menu item in Scottish chip shops, to the **chagrin** of doctors and heart specialists around the world.

**Scotland,
United Kingdom**
Upgraded Candy Bars

What Is Chancaca Syrup?

Chancaca is raw, unrefined, solid cane sugar. One recipe involves melting the chancaca down and adding orange rind, cinnamon, cloves, and water to create the classic syrup. It's a fan-favorite dessert topping in Latin America.

Great Greens

Wasabi Ice Cream

Wasabi is not just a paste to give sushi some extra heat; it's also an ice cream flavor in Japan. Surprisingly edible, wasabi has a tangy taste in this frozen dessert with a lip-tingling effect. Though it's an unlikely flavor, it's not the most outrageous one available. Other Japanese ice cream flavors include eel, black sesame, and squid ink!

Japan, Asia
Hot Ice Cream

Avocado Cream

This is definitely not your standard dish of guacamole. Avocado cream is some Brazilians' favorite way of serving avocados—a simple, light dessert dish that is pretty easy to re-create. Just grab a food processor, one avocado, one teaspoon of lime juice, two tablespoons of sugar, and blend everything well. Then, serve and relish your newfound dessert!

Brazil, South America
All A's

Cendol

Are those . . . green worms? Fear not—*cendol*, Malaysia's favorite chilly dessert, does not get its ingredients from digging in the dirt. Cendol is actually a scrumptious mixture of chewy jelly noodles, coconut milk, palm sugar, and a healthy dose of ice. And the green in the noodles comes from pandan leaves!

 Malaysia, Southeast Asia

Wormed into Our Stomachs

Who Eats the Most Ice Cream?

At one point, Americans were known as the largest consumers of ice cream, but China has crept up in the standings. In 2014, the Chinese enjoyed over 1.6 million gallons of ice cream, while the United States trailed behind with people only eating 1.5 million gallons.

Cendol

 Malaysia, Southeast Asia

Wormed into Our Stomachs

37

Search ≡▾

Unconventional Treats

Sankaya

The best way to picture the *sankaya* is as an inside-out pumpkin pie. A kabocha squash is first hollowed out, and a sweet brew of coconut milk and egg custard is poured in. The entire squash is then steamed to cement the delicious dessert. A popular treat at Thai street stalls, a slice of *sankaya* can be eaten completely— skin, custard, and all!

 Thailand, Southeast Asia
Inside-Out Desserts

Almond Tofu

While the word *tofu* brings to many people's minds bland white cubes, almond tofu is quite a sweet alternative. Commonly found at Chinese dim sum restaurants, almond tofu's texture is similar to jelly. For the most authentic version, try to find almond tofu made from southern Chinese apricot kernels.

 China, Asia
Totally Tofu

38

World's Largest Brownie

In 2014, Canada's McGill University baked a brownie that could feed 20,000 people. Made entirely out of **fair trade** ingredients, this mammoth brownie stretched 30 by 15 feet (9 by 4.5 meters) and weighed around 4,400 pounds (1,996 kilograms). A dedicated team of 20 chefs crafted this overdose of chocolate. The university's collection of hens helped supply more than 8,640 eggs to the cause.

Šakotis

Šakotis is a sweet cake that looks fatal! Though it looks intimidating, this Lithuanian classic is made with simple ingredients. The cake resembles a beige pine tree. To create the cake's "branches," a chef drips batter on a rod inside an oven and rotates the cake at an even pace to build delectable spikes.

Lithuania, Europe
Deadly Delights

Eating Chinese Dim Sum

Traditionally, dim sum is a selection of bite-sized Chinese cuisine served in circle baskets. Dim sum is usually served on carts to each table, making the selection process a fun and interactive experience.

China, Asia
Gimme Some Dim Sum

Meet Heston Blumenthal, Chef & Wizard

Many people call Heston Blumenthal a **culinary** wizard. A British celebrity chef, Blumenthal is known for weaving the science of cooking with a creative flair. He's made bacon-and-egg ice cream, parsnip cereal, and meat fruit. The man is truly the master of delicious **whimsy**!

The Beginning

Born in London on May 27, 1966, Blumenthal did not become invested in the art of food until the age of 16. On a family trip to France, he visited Provence and ate at a Michelin-starred restaurant named *L'Oustau de Baumanière*. He marveled at how the experience awakened all his senses. The smell of lavender, the sight of the server carving lamb, among other details, created a memorable experience for him.

While it was not a lightning-strike moment, from that point forward, Blumenthal began learning more about cooking. He read book after book, building his knowledge and fueling his fascination with the creation of never-been-done-before dishes.

What's a Michelin Star?

The same company that sells tires also awards powerful star ratings to the best restaurants around the world. Anonymous reviewers decide the ratings, on a scale of one to three stars. Three-starred Michelin restaurants are a rare find.

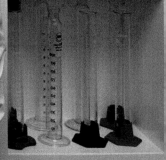

Lickable Wallpaper

In 2010, Blumenthal created rolls of wallpaper that invited guests to lick their way back into the 1960s. The wallpaper was layered with popular 1960s-era food, such as tomato soup and prawn cocktail. It was a huge success with his guests.

Becoming a Name to Remember

Perhaps the most incredible part of Blumenthal's rise to fame is that he has very little "official" training. He spent most of his 20s working odd jobs and studying French cuisine in his spare time. Examining recipes on his own and finding new ways to perfect them became part of his training process.

A defining moment for Blumenthal was reading Harold McGee's *On Food and Cooking*, a book that challenges traditional cooking practices. This caused him to "question everything" he knew, and his inquiring nature is now an important part of his process.

Yes, You Can Eat the Cutlery

A dinner with Blumenthal is never going to be a dull affair. This is especially true when the dessert ends up being the cutlery. During an episode of his cooking TV show *Heston's Feasts*, the chef switched his diners' cutlery to an edible variety, including chocolate spoons!

The Fat Duck

In 1995, Blumenthal took a leap of faith. He purchased a run-down pub in Berkshire, England, and molded it into a bistro. The bistro, named The Fat Duck, first served fairly standard meals, but he slowly began adding menu items that stood out.

Soon, the world began to take notice of this up-and-coming chef, and Blumenthal was awarded his first Michelin star in 1999.

A Costly Meal

Considering a meal at The Fat Duck? You will need a pretty thick wallet to dine there. A ticket to a night of wonder will cost you about £255, or $368—before the tip!

Blumenthal's Signature Dishes

Blumenthal's goal is to create dishes that make the guest feel like a kid in a sweetshop, and his classic creations capture that sentiment perfectly.

Snail Porridge

This is perhaps Blumenthal's most iconic dish, likely because the name "snail porridge" makes ears perk up. While the combination seems ill fated, Blumenthal took deliberate steps to take this porridge from gloopy to good. The oats of the porridge are parsley laced, while the snails are **braised** and buttered, resulting in a finely tuned harmony of flavor.

Bacon-and-Egg Ice Cream

It's breakfast for dessert! Blumenthal's love of exceeding expectations is on full display in this infamous dish. The ice cream is a rich, surprisingly sweet blend of bacon and eggs served with butter caramel, caramelized **brioche**, and jelly tea. Liquid nitrogen is used to create the scrambled look of the "eggs."

bacon-and-egg
ice cream

An Out-of-This-World Bacon Sandwich

Tim Peake, Britain's first official astronaut to spend time in
the International Space Station, was lucky enough to have
Blumenthal create the food for his trip. The creative chef's
greatest challenge was making a bacon sandwich for Peake.
The canned sandwich ended up taking a lot of money and
many months to perfect!

Sounds of the Sea

Another iconic specialty is sounds of the sea. This dish layers the smells and sounds of the ocean in an edible masterpiece. Featuring a **medley** of seafood, the entire dish can be eaten, right down to the white sand. Sounds of the sea is complemented with a music player tucked away in a conch shell. As part of the experience, guests are invited to eat their meals while listening to a symphony of crashing waves and seagulls. Blumenthal's love of a multisensory storytelling experience is clearly evident in this dish!

Meat Fruit

Blumenthal is all about the element of surprise, and creating a dish that jolts and shocks takes time. His famous meat fruit dish is the **epitome** of this attitude, taking 15 hours to complete. Covered in a "peel" made of mandarin jelly, the meat fruit's interior is a sphere of chicken liver and **foie gras**. Meat fruit looks exactly like a juicy fruit, but delights diners with a savory filling, which is part of its undeniable appeal.

Edible Fairy Lights

When entering a world Blumenthal has created, one can never be sure what exactly he has up his sleeve. He has been known to create orange-flavored fairy lights (using jelly and LED lights) to brighten up the atmosphere.

meat fruit

What U.S. Food Should You Try?

Follow this questionnaire, and find out which American state specialty you should try next!

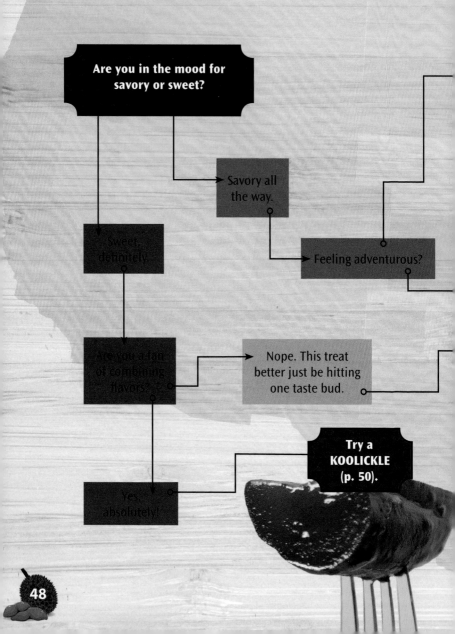

Are you in the mood for savory or sweet?

Savory all the way.

Sweet, definitely.

Feeling adventurous?

Are you a fan of combining flavors?

Nope. This treat better just be hitting one taste bud.

Yes, absolutely!

Try a KOOLICKLE (p. 50).

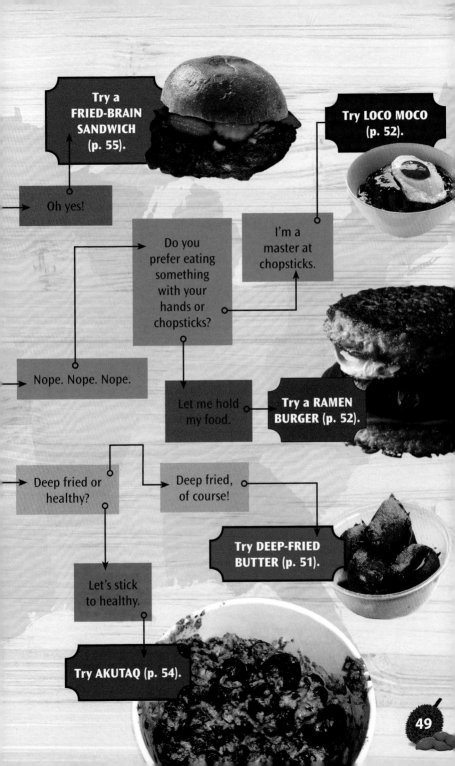

Try a **FRIED-BRAIN SANDWICH** (p. 55).

Oh yes!

Try **LOCO MOCO** (p. 52).

Do you prefer eating something with your hands or chopsticks?

I'm a master at chopsticks.

Nope. Nope. Nope.

Let me hold my food.

Try a **RAMEN BURGER** (p. 52).

Deep fried or healthy?

Deep fried, of course!

Try **DEEP-FRIED BUTTER** (p. 51).

Let's stick to healthy.

Try **AKUTAQ** (p. 54).

Koolickles (Mississippi Delta)

Your love for mixing up flavors has led you to a treat that takes sweet and sour to a whole new level. Koolickles are a Mississippi Delta favorite and are essentially pickles soaked in Kool-Aid® (hence the red color). Combining the two leads to an irresistible sweet and sour flavor, one that you're unlikely to forget!

Koolickles are fairly easy to create at home, as all you need is a jar of pickles, a couple of Kool-Aid packages, some sugar, and a few friends who will also enjoy the flavor combination.

Deep-fry It Up!

You might be surprised at what has been deep-fried and sold as treats across various state fairs in the United States. The following items have all gone into deep fryers and emerged golden: bubblegum, salsa, Twinkies®, pizza, and even alligator!

Deep-Fried Butter (Texas)

Deep-fried butter lives up to its name. Pure butter is whipped into shape, frozen, and then covered in dough before deep-frying. The taste is similar to a biscuit bursting with gooey butter.

Deep-fried butter leapt onto the food scene at the 2009 State Fair of Texas, and since then, the heart-stopping dessert has made its way across the country and even to Canada. While it's not recommended to make deep-fried butter part of your daily diet, the treat might be worth a try!

Average Daily Calories

Country	Calories Consumed (per person)
United States	3,641
Germany	3,539
Japan	2,717
India	2,458
Somalia	1,695

Source: National Geographic

STOP! THINK...

Consider some of the following facts in relation to the chart:

- About 37% of the daily calorie intake for a person in the United States is fats and sugars. How do you think that relates to the obesity epidemic?

- In India, 57% of a person's calorie intake is from grains. How do you think a person in India might react if he or she took the questionnaire on pages 48–49?

- How do you think the calorie intake of the other countries in the chart might compare to the above facts?

Ramen Burger (New York)

Most people are very familiar with burgers, a classic crowd-pleaser on menus across the world. However, the ramen burger poses the question, "What if ramen noodles were used instead of a bread bun?"

This burger **hybrid** is the brainchild of Keizo Shimamoto, a second-generation Japanese American. After quitting his job in finance, Shimamoto moved to Japan to study the art of ramen creation. In 2013, he launched the ramen burger in Brooklyn and won over the stomachs of New Yorkers.

While you might not be near one of Shimamoto's kitchens, ramen burgers are fairly easy to make at home. You'll need ramen, eggs, oil, salt, and pepper. If you're ready to take your burger to the next level, give it a try!

Loco Moco (Hawaii)

In Hawaii, loco moco is comfort food at its finest. Traditionally, loco moco has a base of white rice with a hamburger patty and a sunny-side up egg stacked on top. The final touch is smothering the dish in gravy.

A group of teens at a restaurant in the town of Hilo wanted to eat something different from an American sandwich, something that could be made quickly and cheaply. As the story goes, the crazy dish was named "loco," which means *crazy* in Spanish, and soon "moco" was tagged on because it rhymed so well!

How to Eat Loco Moco

A fun fusion of Asian and Western cuisine, the loco moco is a delight to eat. To get the best of all the flavors, pierce the golden yolk of the egg so it drizzles into the gravy. Then, get a bit of gravy-soaked rice, beef patty, and egg in each bite for the full flavor.

ramen burger

Akutaq (Alaska)

An important part of Alaska's culture, *akutaq* means "mix them together" in Yup'ik and is sometimes referred to as Eskimo ice cream. But this isn't a frozen sweet. The traditional ingredient of akutaq was the fat of Arctic animals, such as moose or caribou. However, the recipe now uses shortening instead, combined with berries and ground fish.

Akutaq is a part of every hunter's travel pack as a nutritious snack. There is no set recipe, though, as each Alaskan family has its own way of creating it. Children often watch their elders so the practice can be passed down generation to generation. If you ever find yourself in Alaska, akutaq is a must-try!

Functional Fat

It might surprise you to know that animal fat has been used in many household items for hundreds of years. It is not simply a part of an animal that can be eaten, it also has numerous other uses. For example, animal fat has been used in the creation of soap, makeup, waterproof garments, and fuel.

Fried-Brain Sandwiches (Midwest)

If you want to try something quite out of the ordinary, head to the states of Indiana, Missouri, or Ohio for sandwiches made with fried pork brains. They come served on hamburger buns and go great with tangy sauces. In the past, these sandwiches were made with beef brains, but fears about mad cow disease have made using that ingredient rarer.

The sandwiches are usually eaten with standard American sides, such as french fries or potato chips. The texture of the brains is creamy once fried, and the taste is rich. Part of the reason for this is that the brains have a high fat content. Biting into it, you taste a crispy, fried chicken-like outside followed by a smooth, custard-like inside. To truly understand, you'll have to try it for yourself!

A Culinary Discovery

This has been quite a wild taste-testing ride through the food world. There have been helpings of green snail porridge, tangy wasabi ice cream, and the crunchy legs of fried spiders. There's been tantalizing street food, super-sweet desserts, and unforgettable culinary inventions. It's been a celebration of the food people love from around the world and a discovery of new items to add to foodie bucket lists.

There is no escaping the fact that what we eat is an important part of who we are. Learning about the food other people eat—the what, why, and how—is vital to understanding more about a country's culture and history. So the next time someone sets down an unfamiliar dish in front of you, embrace the experience! Learn more about the dish's history, where the food is originally from, and who is fond of this particular item. You never know what you will discover.

THINK LINK

It's exciting to incorporate new foods into our diets, but it is always good to remember that you need to populate your plates with food that will keep you healthy.

- © How do people around the world satisfy the many food groups in different ways?

- © Why do people constantly search for new recipes and tastes?

- © What makes a food unique or surprising?

Glossary

array—a selection of items

braised—cooked in fat and stewed in a container

brioche—a sweet bread roll

brittle—easy to crumble or break

chagrin—annoyance

concoction—something made by mixing different things together

cuisine—a unique approach to or type of cooking

culinary—related to cooking

delicacy—a specialty treat

edible—able to be eaten

epitome—an example that perfectly represents something

extract—ingredient in concentrated form

fair trade—a way of trading so that workers in developing countries earn fair prices and receive ethical treatment for their products

ferment—use bacteria to chemically break down food

foie gras—fatty goose liver served as a ground, spreadable paste

hostel—an inexpensive place for travelers to stay overnight

hybrid—combination of two different things

medley—assortment

mundane—dull

perspective—point of view

poutine—a Canadian dish made with french fries and cheese curds and topped with a light brown gravy

puree—a creamy food made out of crushed fruit or vegetables

quinces—acidic fruits typically used for flavoring

quintessential—a perfect example of something

savory—having a spicy or salty taste or smell

scrumptious—very delicious

staple—something common and widespread

unconventional—unusual

whimsy—playful and mischievous

wholly—totally or completely

Index

Check It Out!

Books

Eamer, Claire. 2012. *The World in Your Lunch Box: The Wacky History and Weird Science of Everyday Foods.* Annick Press.

Wishinsky, Frieda, and Elizabeth MacLeod. 2008. *Everything but the Kitchen Sink: Weird Stuff You Didn't Know About Food.* Scholastic.

Zemser, Amy Bronwen. 2008. *Dear Julia.* Greenwillow Books.

Zimmern, Andrew. 2012. *Andrew Zimmern's Field Guide to Exceptionally Weird, Wild, & Wonderful Foods.* Feiwel and Friends.

Video

Zimmern, Andrew. *Bizarre Foods with Andrew Zimmern.* Travel Channel. http://www.travelchannel.com/shows /bizarre-foods/video.

Websites

National Geographic. *What the World Eats.* http://www .nationalgeographic.com/what-the-world-eats/.

TIME Magazine. *Hungry Planet: What the World Eats.* http://time.com/8515/what-the-world-eats-hungry -planet/.

Try It!

You are the chef of a new restaurant in your hometown called *Unusual Eats*. What type of menu will you create? How will you craft each dish so that it is either delicious or adventurous? You've got some decisions to make:

- Draw a logo or write a slogan for your restaurant.
- Decide what kinds of dishes will be included on your menu.
- Decide which dishes will serve as appetizers, main courses, and dessert options.
- Plan which ingredients will make each dish unique and delicious, and list them. Try to incorporate ingredients from around the world.
- Think about a memorable name for each dish. Does the name reflect the main ingredients in a fun and engaging way? How will each dish stand out on your menu as strange or surprising?

About the Author

Monika Davies is a Canadian writer and a big believer in trying all types of food, especially while traveling. She has eaten frog legs in Vietnam, drunk goat milk in Mongolia, and devoured every kind of dessert she can get her hands on. If you told her she could either have a lifetime supply of tiramisu or the power of invisibility, she would choose tiramisu—every time.

Davies graduated from the University of British Columbia with a bachelor of fine arts in creative writing.

Table of Contents

The Surprising Food We Love

Food is an important ingredient in the recipe for human survival. Every person needs to eat food, but that doesn't mean it has to be a **mundane** task. People around the world have come up with various ways to ward off hunger pangs, and the results can sometimes be spicy . . . and unique!

There is a story behind every piece of food. The food we choose to eat and enjoy tells us a lot about who we are, the cultural influences in our lives, and what we value. In this book, we will peek into grocery stores in different countries, glimpse some surprising street food, and head into the kitchen of a celebrity chef known for his unique creations. Let's bite into the world of *"can you really eat that?"* with gusto. Jump in and discover the stories behind the surprising foods that people love around the world!